FARM ANIMALS

Geese

by Hollie Endres

BELLWETHER MEDIA • MINNEAPOLIS, MN

Note to Librarians, Teachers, and Parents:

Blastoff! Readers are carefully developed by literacy experts and combine standards-based content with developmentally-appropriate text.

Level 1 provides the most support through repetition of high-frequency words, light text, predictable sentence patterns, and strong visual support.

Level 2 offers early readers a bit more challenge through varied simple sentences, increased text load, and less repetition of high frequency words.

Level 3 advances early-fluent readers toward fluency through increased text and concept load, less reliance on visuals, longer sentences, and more literary language.

Level 4 builds reading stamina by providing more text per page, increased use of punctuation, greater variation in sentence patterns, and increasingly challenging vocabulary.

Level 5 encourages readers to move from "learning to read" to "reading to learn" by providing even more text, varied writing styles, and less familiar topics.

Whichever book is right for your reader, Blastoff! Readers are the perfect books to build confidence and encourage a love of reading that will last a lifetime!

This edition first published in 2008 by Bellwether Media.

No part of this publication may be reproduced in whole or in part without written permission of the publisher. For information regarding permission, write to Bellwether Media Inc., Attention: Permissions Department, Post Office Box 1C, Minnetonka, MN 55345-9998.

Library of Congress Cataloging-in-Publication Data
Endres, Hollie J.
  Geese / by Hollie J. Endres.
    p. cm. – (Blastoff! readers. Farm Animals)
Summary: "A basic introduction to geese and how they live on the farm. Simple text and full color photographs. Developed by literacy experts for students in kindergarten through third grade"–Provided by publisher.
  Includes bibliographical references and index.
  ISBN-13: 978-1-60014-084-6 (hardcover : alk. paper)
  ISBN-10: 1-60014-084-X (hardcover : alk. paper)
  1. Geese–Juvenile literature. I. Title.

SF505.3.E536 2008
636.5'98–dc22   2007007464

Contents

Geese are birds. Some live in the **wild**. Some live on farms. One of these birds by itself is called a goose.

Geese feathers
can be white,
gray, brown
or black.

Geese have **webbed** feet. This helps geese **paddle** in water.

webbed feet

Geese **waddle** when they walk on land.

Geese have a
hard **bill**.
They use their bill
to pick up food.

bill

13

Geese eat plants.
They help farmers
by eating **weeds**
around the farm.

Geese honk.
They also hiss
to chase other
animals away.

17

Geese live in
a group called
a **gaggle**.
They stay
together.

Geese follow
each other
around the farm.

Glossary

bill—the hard mouth of a bird

gaggle—a group of geese

paddle—to move through water using arms, legs, or a tool; geese use their feet to paddle.

waddle—to walk with short steps and the body swaying back and forth

webbed—being connected by skin

weeds—plants that farmers do not like; weeds grow quickly and crowd out other plants.

wild—living in nature

To Learn More

AT THE LIBRARY

Braun, Trudi. *My Goose Betsy*. Cambridge, Mass.: Candlewick, 1999.

Provenson, Alice and Martin Provenson. *Our Animals Friends at Maple Hill Farm*. New York: Aladdin, 2001.

Schuh, Mari C. *Geese on the Farm*. Mankato, Minn.: Capstone Press, 2003.

ON THE WEB

Learning more about farm animals is as easy as 1, 2, 3.

1. Go to www.factsurfer.com

2. Enter "farm animals" into search box.

3. Click the "Surf" button and you will see a list of related web sites.

With factsurfer.com, finding more information is just a click away.

Index

The photographs in this book are reproduced through the courtesy of: Haihong Zhao, front cover; Dana Tezarr/ Getty Images, p. 5; Johan Swanepoel, p. 7; Stephen Krasemann/Getty Images, p. 9; Hongwu Wang, p. 11; goran cakmazovic, p. 13; Daniel Gale, p. 15; Georgette Douwma/Getty Images, p. 17; Robert W. Ahrens, p. 19; Marilyn Barbone, p. 21.